✠

WINCHESTER

Other titles available in this series

PILGRIM · GUIDE

WINCHESTER

Michael Till

Illustrated by
Jill Bentley

CANTERBURY
PRESS
Norwich

Text © Michael Till 1997
Illustrations © Jill Bentley 1997

First published in 1997 by The Canterbury Press Norwich
(a publishing imprint of Hymns Ancient & Modern Limited
a registered charity)
St Mary's Works, St Mary's Plain
Norwich, Norfolk NR3 3BH

Michael Till has asserted his right under the Copyright, Designs and
Patents Act 1988, to be identified as Author of this Work

British Library Cataloguing in Publication Data

A catalogue record for this book is available
from the British Library

ISBN 1-85311-181-3

Typeset, printed and bound in Great Britain by
The Lavenham Press Ltd,
Lavenham, Suffolk, CO10 9RN

Contents

A part of the Pilgrim's Way known as The Nuns' Walk, Kingsworthy, near Winchester.

A Personal Introduction

I don't know how you came to Winchester or why. I came here from Canterbury and I walked. Although I was leaving one job for another, I decided to make the journey as a pilgrim – along the ancient route from Winchester to Canterbury but in the opposite direction. With every mile I was taking leave of my old diocese and the people among whom I had worked and walking to a new place. I would be a stranger dependent on the goodwill of unknown others but I knew that the God who had moved me on would also be where I was going.

How about you? Even if you are just on a day trip and want to be taken out of yourself a little, I believe you will find something here that speaks to you. Your visit will turn out to have had something of the pilgrimage about it, even if you might not use that word yourself.

The volunteers on duty at Winchester are welcoming to pilgrims like you and me. You will recognise them by their badges. Question them and you catch something of their own very personal experience of the cathedral. When I have been here longer I too will know the Cathedral as only a resident can – in the ever-changing light and varying moods and seasons. But this is a guide written by a newly-arrived pilgrim like yourself. I hope that you, like me, decide you were right to come.

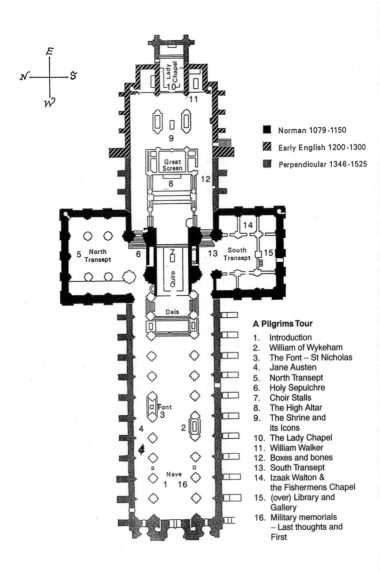

Norman 1079-1150

Early English 1200-1300

Perpendicular 1346-1525

E

N — S

W

Lady Chapel

11

9

Great Screen

8

12

5 North Transept

6

7 Quire

13

South Transept

14

15

Dais

Font 3

2

4

Nave

1 16

A Pilgrims Tour

2

Arriving and Beginning

Some have been swept in through the Great West Doors with the sound of trumpets. But you can sit quietly for a moment before making your way to the heart of the cathedral. A most famous arrival in Winchester was that of William the Conqueror. He came to the Old Minster, the ground plan of which you can see laid out in the grass to the north of the cathedral. As a deliberate statement of kingship he wore his crown – not the modest band with the fleur-de-lis of his Saxon predecessor, but the extravagant work of a Greek craftsman, covered with Arabian gold and Egyptian gems. Sit and look at the Cathedral for a moment and think of that arrival.

The Coming of a Conqueror

Winchester was the capital of Alfred's kingdom of Wessex and a major treasury of the kings of England. William, crowned and surrounded by his barons and by churchmen, was the Norman Conqueror claiming his place as King of England. His dramatic entrance into the Old Minster was designed not only to convince his Saxon subjects that they were under his rule but also to impress the collection of neighbours and adventurers that we call the Normans and to give them a shared identity. Later, those same Normans would find a new identity as the English, but the story has its beginnings here.

As a royal treasury, Winchester needed to be held securely. This was well understood by William's younger son, Henry. When his brother William Rufus, William II, died in the New Forest in a hunting incident, he raced to Winchester without even stopping to view the body, secured the treasure and hastened to London to be made king. Successive bishops of Winchester were appointed Chancellor or Treasurer to oversee the treasury. We can understand why, during the period of civil war under Stephen, both sides should be so anxious to secure Winchester for themselves.

The Church was important to William. It provided a kind of educated civil service, invaluable in bringing the Domesday Book – the survey of William's kingdom – into its final form. The church also provided knights and soldiers which the feudal system required of great landowners. William had been generous to the Church in Normandy, but it was a church which was reformed, well-educated and faithful to its calling. Under the influence of Lanfranc – formerly Abbot of Bec and then of William's new foundation in Caen – the English Church too experienced the bracing wind of reform and reorganisation. Winchester's Bishop, Stigand – also Archbishop of Canterbury – was one of the first to go. Stigand had held both posts with the agreement of the Pope but not, unfortunately, the one of the two competing Popes supported by William. Lanfranc became Archbishop of Canterbury and a relative of William's, Walkelin, was appointed Bishop of Winchester. This Cathedral is in origin Walkelin's building.

Most gracious Father, we most humbly beseech thee for thy holy Catholic Church. Fill it with all truth; in all truth with all peace. Where it is corrupt, purge it; where it is in error, direct it; where anything is amiss, reform it; where it is right, strengthen and confirm it; where it is in want, furnish it; where it is divided, heal it and unite it in thy love; through Jesus Christ Our Lord, AMEN.

William Laud, Archbishop of Canterbury (1573-1645)

On the Way with Walkelin – The Nave

Until the 'Gothic' Liverpool Cathedral was built this century, some said Winchester, measuring 169 metres, was the longest Gothic cathedral in Europe and others maintained it had the longest Gothic nave. But what was it for, this great building? The two to three thousand townsfolk of Winchester at that time had fifty churches to choose from and were bound to attend their parish church. The major showpiece events for church, court or city were sporadic. Some airily suggest that the builders were trying to buy their way into heaven. But Lanfranc and William knew they couldn't earn or buy the mercy of God. William Wordsworth wrote a fine sonnet about King's College Chapel, Cambridge, which has a point for us here:

> Tax not the royal saint with vain expense,
> With ill-matched aims the Architect who planned -
> Albeit labouring for a scanty band
> Of white-robed Scholars only – this immense
> And glorious Work of fine intelligence!
> Give all thou canst; high Heaven rejects the law
> Of nicely calculated less or more.

You may think that the scale of the Cathedral is excessive, that the means far outweigh the ends. But as you walk further inside, quietly entering into its story, you may decide that even this building is outdone by the extravagance of God's love for us.

Just before we move on, look at the vault and the string courses across the top of the arches which stride down both sides of the Nave. You will see there the arms of Bishop Edyngton and of William of Wykeham who both refashioned this Nave, and the white hart with chained collar, badge of Richard II. But you will also find faces and figures tucked away in corners. Do they represent people the carver knew? Or are these the individuals who built this place?

William of Wykeham

Cardinal Beaufort

William of Waynflete

The Builders of Winchester – the Tomb of William of Wykeham

Come half way down the Nave. On the right hand side you will see, enclosed by a finely-carved Gothic screen, the tomb chest of William of Wykeham, angels at his head and small figures of priests at his feet. At the foot of the tomb is an altar with niches for saints above it. Reformers removed the saints but they have been replaced by these young models in fancy dress.

William of Wykeham's vision is dominant in the Nave. William was a local boy, educated at the High School. He rose to become a powerful Chancellor of the Exchequer, Chief Keeper and Surveyor for much of the king's building work including Windsor Castle. He is also remembered for his own 'double foundation' of Winchester College (just outside the city wall on the south side of the Cathedral) and New College, Oxford.

The Founder's Charter for 'St Mary College of Winchester' of 20 October 1382 conveys a perhaps pardonable sense of William's achievements: '…brought forth into this vale of misery, wretched and naked… [God who] on occasion places the humble on high… has enriched us, undeserving as we are with great honours, … raised us beyond our worth to various positions of rank'. His college was for seventy poor and needy scholars (such as he had been?) and 'for the upholding, exaltation and advancement of faith and church and the increase of liberal arts and sciences'.

On the south side of the South Aisle (beyond the Chantry and a bit further back towards the West End) you will find a fine memorial by Flaxman which shows Dr Warton teaching four little boys across the road at Winchester College. Then as you make your way down the North Aisle to the North Transept you will see little wooden benches with pointed ends on which the boys sat and where they have carved their names.

You may like to reflect upon the idea of education. William of Wykeham and his contemporaries believed that whichever branch of knowledge is pursued, they all converge on a single universe of knowledge which ultimately expresses the mind and purposes of God. This is the origin of the word 'university'. Today specialists seem to grow further and further away from each other. And whereas learning was once advocated for its 'usefulness', does it now risk being occupational therapy for the private pleasure of people who have no other use for it?

O God the Holy Spirit, who art the author of all good and the giver of all wisdom, bestow on us thy servants the power of learning, the desire of wisdom and grace to do good; that by an honest life and prudent conduct we may be found worthy to serve thee and thy kingdom, who livest and reignest God for ever and ever. AMEN.

Dr Caius' prayers for daily use in his College

Chantry Chapels

Chantry chapels – in which dignitaries were buried – are a very special feature of this Cathedral. A priest would have said mass here for the soul of the departed William. William may have drawn attention to his own successes but he knew his need of prayer.

Isn't this too a reason why this Cathedral was built and the monks sang their offices in the choir day and night? Our world needs the sustained offering of prayer, that continuing rise as of woodsmoke, as it also needs the continuing mercy of God, which has been likened to the falling of soft rain or the silent coming of the dew.

We need it too. There is such a contrast between God's justice and our way with each other, God's truth and our approximate veracity, God's mercy and our occasional kindness, God's peace and the reluctant compromises and smouldering aggression of our human affairs. Let us offer prayer ourselves and be thankful for God's mercy.

O God of our Fathers, who of old didst move thy servants in this place to build an house of prayer for the offering of eternal praises to thy glorious majesty: Grant to us, and to all who herein call upon thy holy name from age to age, that, by the offering of our lives and the praises of our lips, we may ever seek the welfare of thy glory and thy kingdom; through Jesus Christ our Lord. AMEN.

Prayer of Winchester Cathedral

The tomb of William of Wykeham

The Font

Now cross the Aisle and turn towards the west as if you were going out of the Cathedral again but on the north side. As you go, look up at the window on the north side which shows King George VI (George V faces him in an equivalent window on the south side) and his queen, Elizabeth. Above them, looking like actors in a melodramatic repertory company, are Henry IV and the wife he married here, Joan of Navarre.

Continue along the North Aisle in a westward direction and there, on your left hand side, with little candles burning before it, is the Font. It's a curious piece, rather crudely carved, made from a piece of black marble from Tournai – one of a group of seven which came to this country from Belgium. The belief is that it was brought here by Henry of Blois, bishop when his brother Stephen and the Empress Matilda were warring over the English throne, and still bishop under Stephen's successor Henry II.

This black stone has a strangely primitive presence. It seems reminiscent of a sacrificial stone, more associated with blood than water. Since we are baptised into the death and resurrection of Christ, does that ambiguity matter?

The carving on the Font is crude and simple. Two sides show incidents from the legend of St Nicholas; the third side depicts doves pecking grapes (symbolic of Christians being fed by Christ who said, 'I am the true vine'); on the fourth side are two doves and a lion or possibly a salamander. One of the Nicholas carvings shows the saint giving three bags of gold to three girls for their marriage dowries in order to save them from prostitution. A suitor looks on. The other

Nicholas carving illustrates the tale of three boys, killed by a wicked landlord, who were raised to life by the saint. The three gentlemen in the boat may be the Turkish sailors legend says he saved.

Saved by St Nicholas.

This is one of the two important iconographic cycles of Nicholas's life, the other being on an ivory crozier head at the Victoria and Albert Museum. Not much fact is known of Nicholas and much is legendary. However this prayer to Nicholas by St Anselm – sometime a pupil of Lanfranc and, under physical duress, made Archbishop of Canterbury at the time of Rufus – may help us. It was written shortly before the Tournai font came to Winchester:

> …but my sins are without bounds or limits,
> my prayer will not be heard,
> all this is not enough without an intercessor.
> I will pray to one of the great friends of God
> and perhaps God will hear him on my behalf.

I will call upon Nicholas, that great confessor,
whose name is honoured throughout the world.
Nicholas!
If only he will hear me!
Great Nicholas!

But stop for a moment longer and reflect upon the Font.
Were you brought to baptism? If so, you should surely be
glad that someone wanted you to be 'dunked in the love of
God'. Say 'thank you' for them. Or maybe you are a god-
parent, an aunt or uncle and there's some young person for
whom you want to pray. Here are two prayers. Light a
candle if you wish and leave it to continue burning after
you've gone.

*Thank you for those who cared for us, those who wished us well and
those who influenced us for good. If we are what you and they
intend, you will know. If we are not, forgive us and guide us. But
let that not be to their charge. Thank you for them. Keep them in
your love as they kept us in theirs. AMEN.*

And here's a prayer ascribed to St Aethelwold, a 10th century
Bishop of Winchester:

*We beseech thee O God, open thy heavens in mercy upon the soul
of thy servant… May thy gifts descend upon him. Put forth thine
own hand from heaven and touch his head. May he feel the touch
of thine hand and receive the joy of thy Holy Spirit, that he may
remain blessed for evermore. AMEN.*

R.I.P. – the Memorials of the Nave Aisles

Before moving on, stand and see how many memorials there are along the walls of the North and South Nave Aisles. Some of the ledger stones – as those large flooring slabs are called – have very simple inscriptions. Some have a story or an idle-curiosity factor. It pleases me that in front of the Nave Altar there is a slab for a Dr Mirth Wafferer who married the daughter of Sir Peter Wroth.

You will see many memorials for Army officers. We will look at the memorials for Regiments later on. But note on this North Aisle the memorial to two members of the Gough family, father and son, who both won the VC. Or see, underneath his banner which draws attention to the place, the inscription to the first Earl Wavell, Field Marshal and Viceroy of India, who died in 1950 and is buried in the Garth of Winchester College Cloister. Maybe you know his collection of the poems he had come to value, *Other Men's Flowers*. For a soldier with his career I like the inscription

And glory is the least of things
That follow this man home.

Some of the inscriptions suggest that heaven was getting a bargain! However I suspect a sneaky touch of honesty when someone, having described a clergyman fulsomely, says his wife 'endured 50 years of happy marriage'. And what was Chaloner Ogle doing all his life that, by the age of 90, he was still said to have an unblemished character?

See how many of them are anxious to tell you who married whom and just how smart their social connections really were. Few memorials are as inflated as that to the Rivers family in the Epiphany Chapel. Then seek out the ledger-stone to **Jane Austen**, a little further down the North Aisle towards the West Door. She died here in Winchester and, as you can see, her ledger-stone gives no indication that she was a writer. The brass plate on the wall was added later, and even later, a window above that. Jane Austen saw beneath the pompous phrases and the flourishes and fashions behind which we try to conceal ourselves, and perceived the painful, inside stories of people like ourselves.

Stop here for a while and then, taking her honesty with you, travel on towards the east.

Thank you for writers and those who see beneath the skin and show us that we are not so different from one another. We all need your forgiveness. When we are pompous, of your goodness dent our dignity that we may recover our common humanity which you have made your own in Jesus Christ our Lord. AMEN.

The North Transept

Moving east towards the High Altar, you will come to the North Transept. This Transept, stretching north and south of the main line of the Cathedral, forms the arms of the cross which is its ground plan. You can see here how solidly, how massively, the Normans built and form some idea of the huge areas of stone that had to be cut away to give the pillars and arches of the Nave their present, more elegant, form.

By the time they had built to first-floor level it seems that the idea of building towers at the outer extremities of the Transepts had been formed. You can see where preparations were made in the building of the next and subsequent levels. But then the towers were never built. Why?

Ask a guide to point out to you where, at the ends of the Transepts, the builders planned to build towers. Then turn round and look at the vast piers which support the central Tower and connect the North Transept to the body of the Cathedral. It is said that these are the most massive tower piers in any cathedral in this country. The masonry and jointing is of a finer quality than the fairly rough, heavy masonry of some other parts of this North Transept. And all of this is to be explained by the fact that Walkelin's original main tower collapsed.

William Rufus was buried beneath it and, to the popular mind, the collapse was a sign of God's judgement on him, some seven years after his death in 1100. One chronicler solemnly states that it 'was a grievous wrong to bury in the sacred place one who all his life had been profane and sensual and who died without the Christian viaticum'. It was from stories of such disasters, and there were more than we commonly suppose, that master masons learned.

Here at Winchester the masons were exceedingly cautious in the aftermath. Elsewhere more elegant solutions were found. At Ely the tower put up by Walkelin's brother, Abbot Simeon, collapsed after 200 years, demolishing the chancel as well. The Ely master mason, Alan of Walsingham, gave up entirely the notion of a central tower and created a sequence of springing arches which meet to create a lantern above the centre of the crossing. Or do you know Wells where the arches of the nave threatened to buckle and were given that magical, hourglass bracing? Or Canterbury where the arches, again too tall for their own good, had decorated bracing inserted to keep the pillars from buckling?

Are we to find a pilgrim reflection out of this? Making a life and mending a life may make us sympathetic to the builders and what they achieved. Some folk will be heartened by the Winchester solution – nothing fancy, nothing clever, but good, solid stone not to be shaken. Or is there something here about the way we over-reach ourselves, then have to rethink, redesign, come up with some way of coping with an unexpected weakness? What joy if we can find a wonderful, elegant and inventive solution. But let's not be ungrateful for the unimaginative solution here either. At least the Tower is still standing.

O Lord God, when thou givest to thy servants to endeavour any great matter, grant us also to know that it is not the beginning, but the continuing of the same, until it be thoroughly finished, which yieldeth the true glory; through him who for the finishing of thy work laid down his life for us, our Redeemer, Jesus Christ. AMEN.
Prayer after Sir Francis Drake

The North Transept.

Rest in the Sepulchre

Now turn and look south again and you will see an arch with an arched doorway to one side of it opening on to a small chapel, which is probably in darkness. Walk up to that open archway and, at one end of the tomb that lies across the archway you are looking through, you will find a white press button which will bring on the lights. This the Chapel of the Holy Sepulchre.

The reason for its name is clear enough. Behind the altar, on the east wall of the chapel you will see a wall painting showing Christ being taken down from the cross and then being laid in the tomb. Here we bring the consecrated bread and wine from the service at which we remember the Last Supper on what is called Maundy Thursday. It remains here through Good Friday, when we remember Christ's crucifixion and until Easter Day when we celebrate his rising again.

The painting itself was only disclosed in the 1960s when restorers were working on a later wall painting which had been applied over it. That later painting – essentially the same scene – was removed and placed at the opposite end of the Chapel. There too, Christ is being laid in the tomb, his Mother is at his side and an angel, to the left, is pointing this out to the two Maries who have come to the tomb.

At the extreme right hand edge of the painting behind the altar is a barely legible detail of a subject later developed in a painting on the wall facing you. It illustrates the so-called Harrowing of Hell, a story which goes back to a very ancient but apocryphal work called the *Acts of Pilate*.

The story begins in the hours following Christ's death when as yet all our ancestors were shut up in Hell. Do you

18

believe in Hell? It doesn't matter. This Hell is the condition of being separated from God and hopelessly regretting so much that we did in the past which might have seemed reasonable at the time. But then come mysterious voices instructing the eternal accusers to release those they mock and torment so relentlessly. Why? Because someone is coming who will break down the doors which shut them in. And it is Christ, carrying the cross, who rescues those who were tormented and takes them into his paradise.

As they are all about to leave Hell, following Jesus, Adam points out that others will come to that place of despair after them and will not know where to go. 'So, Lord,' he asks, 'will you leave your cross here to point the way we have gone that they may come to your place also?'

The old story of Adam and Eve which began so promisingly ended with them being turned out of Paradise as a judgement on them for disobeying God. That had seemed to be that. But where they were once tormented and tormenting themselves (is there any difference?), they find their story taken into the story of how God sets out to redeem his people through Christ. A narrative about failure becomes a narrative about God's grace and a new beginning.

Remember those who have died and who were close to you. Maybe there are episodes in your family's past for which you still harbour a regret, the thought of something still unfulfilled or resolved. Offer such stories here, leave them here, confident that Christ's cross does gather them into his story and heal them. You may like to use this prayer:

Almighty God, before whose face the generations rise and pass away, the strength of those who labour and the repose of those who rest: we humbly commend the soul of thy servants into thy hands as into the hands of a faithful Creator and merciful Saviour. Grant them thy peace, may light perpetual shine upon them and in thy loving wisdom and almighty power work in them the good purpose of thy perfect will, through Jesus Christ our Lord. AMEN.

Christ is buried. 12th century version.

Carpentry and Canticles – The Quire Stalls

Walk up the steps, turn right through the doorway into the Quire and come down to stand between the Quire Stalls which, as you can see, are made of wood, finely carved. A good craftsman can teach us something about grace – having the right implement for the hand, and a hand expertly able to respond to the mind, or even to discover (such is the nature of skill) a possibility that the mind has not yet discerned. If you have bodged a piece of work or seen a craftsman, with grace and elegance, achieve it, you will savour this craftsmanship and remember again the meaning of that familiar prayer:

Jesus, Master Carpenter of Nazareth, who on the cross through wood and nails didst work man's whole salvation: wield well thy tools in this thy workshop; that we who come to thee rough-hewn may by thy hand be fashioned to a truer beauty and a greater usefulness; for the honour of thy Holy Name. AMEN.

Where Earth and Heaven Meet

The instrument of so much grace here in the Quire was someone called William of Lingwood, who came from Norfolk. See the different forms of foliage he carved – oak-leaves, beech-leaves, hazel, alchemilla, plane, geranium. See the faces – faces of dignitaries perhaps. There are two kings, one of them Edward I and his two wives Eleanor of Castile and Margaret of France, and the other Edward II with his wife Isabella, known as 'the she-wolf'. Here too in this luxuriant foliage are the strange creatures of the woodlands and the Green Man himself.

From time to time we catch hints of a primitive religion still lurking, half seen. What are we to make of the anthropologists' suggestion that William Rufus, killed in the New Forest, was the necessary sacrifice of the ailing King in some such cult? Our predecessors certainly believed that there were forces not tamed by the Church which might yet leap out on the unwary. Yet the predominant impression here is neither deference to grandees, nor anxiety about primitive forces, but sheer joy and exuberance of life and enjoyment of the skill to depict it.

Misericord – support for tired monks.

Beneath the seats, which fold up, are the wonderfully carved misericords – those little shelf-seats where a monk, tired of standing, might hitch himself, take the weight off his feet. There is a mermaid with a comb and a mirror, a king's head and a person putting his tongue out and an old woman spinning with a cat nearby, a man fighting a wild animal, another Green Man and various mythical monsters with which our ancestors used to frighten themselves and each other.

Astonishingly this burgeoning, happy and sometimes bucolic panorama of life provided the setting for the regular offering of the eight monastic 'hours' of prayer – Lauds, Prime, Terce, Sext, None, Vespers, Compline and Mattins. These services were composed of psalms, hymns, lessons, antiphons, responses and versicles and prayers. It seems good that the place of prayer has such rich reminders of the world for which prayer is made.

The Lord Will Come to his Temple – the Lectern and Pulpit

Now, come back towards the Altar, to the gangway which crosses the Quire. Look to east and west and then back again. To the east lies the Altar, the place where the bread is broken and distributed. To the west is the Lectern where the Bible is kept and, beyond the wooden screen on the north side of the Quire, the Pulpit. These are both places where, as we say, the Word is broken (expounded) and distributed ('fed' to the congregation). As the English Reformation proceeded, the Cathedral passed from the care of those who believed that Christ gives himself pre-eminently through the bread broken, into the hands of those who believed he gives himself pre-eminently through the Word. Now, in our own day, we break the bread and the Word together: the Church is both Catholic and Reformed.

Take a step or two towards the Altar. As you pass the Bishop's Quire Throne which is on the south – that is to say your right-hand side, you will see a small memorial on the wall to **Bishop Lancelot Andrewes**. He was born at the end of Mary Tudor's reign and lasted almost until the end of the reign of James I – living between the most troublesome times. He helped create the distinctive Anglican theology – neither rigidly Protestant nor slavishly Catholic but, in the view of many, sharing the best attributes of both. It was his preaching, we are told, that was so influential but we have his prayers – often given exaggerated respect, but nonetheless spacious in style, generous in spirit and honest in their devotion. Here is one of them:

God, our Father, let us find grace in thy sight, so as to have grace to serve thee acceptably with reverence and godly fear; and further grace not to receive thy grace in vain, nor to neglect it and fall from it but to stir it up and go in it and so persevere in it unto the end of our lives; through Jesus Christ our Lord. AMEN.

The Great Screen

Now take up a position facing the High Altar but a few yards away from the rail. Look at the Great Screen behind the Altar. If we wanted to be sniffy about it we could say that we are looking at the scene of a double desecration: the first by destruction, the second by restoration.

The Screen with its original figures was constructed, it is thought, during the time of Bishop William of Waynflete whose Chantry Chapel you will see later. It has close similarities with the screen at St Albans. The sculpted figures that were originally put here have been dated to between 1475 and 1490.

The first desecration was worked by the reformers who came here in 1538 and tore the original figures from the alcoves in the Screen. It is hard to believe that those destroyers thought themselves agents of God, asserting true religion and abolishing superstition and idolatry, but they did. What may have seemed like an advance to them leaves the rest of us feeling deprived.

Later, when we come to that point in our tour, if you make your way to the Triforium Gallery in the South Transept, you will find such figures of that earlier period as have been recovered. The hand and hammer and chisel of the sculptor have left us with figures that have life and real loveliness. There is a Virgin and Child, so badly broken, yet still not seeming to be mere stone, but a living presence, caught between one breath and the next. You can imagine a hot-eyed reformer arguing that simple people were falling in love with images instead of God.

Maybe these figures were among the last representatives

of a spiritual devotion which was almost exhausted by 1538, though to many of us in our time, it again has real value. But these figures come from an earlier time when what you could call 'the way of imagination and compassionate devotion' was a way into deeper faith. Such an approach begins simply enough. Imagine you are a mother standing by while your son dies; imagine how she feels his pain! Or imagine you are Peter, the disciple, who has just denied Jesus as he is about to undergo his trial and death. These figures provide rich material for telling and retelling stories from the Bible or from the lives of saints or notorious sinners, all to bring people to a deeper faith.

But you would not claim that the detail you imagine is necessarily true; you might, for example, imagine Peter's denial taking place in the courtyard outside the Great Hall at the top of the High Street. Of course it didn't, but that image may help you to have a more vivid awareness of what was going on for Peter and Jesus in that story and what it means for you.

However what begins as an aid to faith becomes a danger to it if the details supplied by the imagination become treated as further fact to be believed. The reformers who destroyed these figures may have felt that the truth of the Gospel had become buried beneath a vast edifice of superstitious and false beliefs which needed clearing away. These lovely figures were casualties in a conflict which did no credit to the Church.

The Victorian 'Restoration'

As an inscription on the wall on the south side of the South Presbytery Aisle records, the Victorian 'restoration' of the Screen was begun in commemoration of the Venerable Philip Jacob, Archdeacon, with some sense of audacity. The back of the Screen carries a notice giving the names of donors and which figures they paid for. It was clearly a spirited community effort although the total effect may seem a bit dull. Some of the characters depicted will be strange to us, like St Grimbald, donated by someone called H. Little-hales Esq. Others are more familiar like the saintly Bishop Ken, donated by the Sunday Schools of the Diocese. The restoration programme was completed in 1899.

The later sculptures of the restoration (some would say 'second desecration') are by contrast careful pieces showing the artist's model as St Cecilia or a respectable middle-class gentleman barely disguised by the habit of a bishop or a king. It was a good try and better than nothing, but that's about it. The devotional background just wasn't there.

Whatever we think of the appearance of this screen, we have at last come to the heart of the medieval cathedral. Here people came seeking the same love God showed to us when, in Christ, he came to take us to himself. Here they received Christ who came to them again in the form of bread and wine. Here they believed they worshipped with the Church visible and invisible, and the figures on the screen were a reminder of the invisible Church, singing the same canticle of praise. That's why our order of service says:

Therefore with angels and archangels, and with all the company of heaven,
we laud and magnify thy glorious name, evermore praising thee and saying ,
'Holy, holy, holy, Lord God of hosts,
heaven and earth are full of thy glory...
Hosanna in the highest'.

Wherefore seeing we also are compassed about with so great a cloud of witnesses, let us lay aside every weight and the sin which doth so easily beset us, and let us run with patience the race that is set before us, looking unto Jesus the author and finisher of our faith; who for the joy that was set before him endured the cross, despising the shame, and is set down at the right hand of the throne of God.

Epistle to the Hebrews 12:1-2

A Flock of Pelicans

Before moving on, reflect for a moment on a favourite image of our predecessors here – that of the pelican in her nest, feeding her young. You'll find her carved at the foot of the cross on which Christ hangs. It was believed that the pelican fed her young with blood from her own breast and so she became a symbol of Christ feeding us with his own flesh and blood. This 'Pelican in her Piety' is a sermon in stone about the offering of bread and wine, Christ's body and blood, made daily at this altar.

'The Pelican in her Piety' from Bishop Fox's Chantry.

Honoured on High – the Roof Bosses above the High Altar

In a marvellous twist, our notions of honour are turned topsy-turvy by the bosses on the roof above the High Altar. Unlike the shields and badges elsewhere in the Cathedral, which speak of the honour given to somebody or other, these blazons record the *dis*honour done to Christ. (There's a mirror on a trolley which you can wheel round to help you see them). You can see for example the man who spat in Jesus's face, and the jug and the basin with which Pilate washed his hands of responsibility for his death. You can see the three dice with which the soldiers gambled for his robe.

These marks of Christ's dishonour show us paradoxically why we honour him: they are evidence of his love for us. This prayer of St Richard of Chichester takes up that theme in a spirit of thanksgiving:

Thanks be to thee O Lord Jesus Christ, for all the benefits which thou hast given us, for the pains and insults thou hast borne for us. O Most Merciful Redeemer, Friend and Brother, may I know thee more clearly, love thee more dearly and follow thee more nearly, day by day. AMEN.

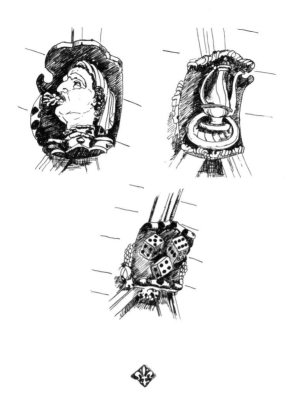

This is the High Altar of this Cathedral. You will see other altars and once there would have been even more. In the days when they were all frequently in use, the common folk came in and, milling around in the Nave where there were no chairs, heard the monks singing their services. But if a bell tinkled to announce that the bread and wine had been consecrated, they would come to the altars, some running, to look on the miracle. They would be running to meet the Lord who had so graciously come to meet them.

The Retroquire

Now leave the Quire, left or right it doesn't matter, and carry on towards the east of the Cathedral. You will pass another chantry, either Bishop Fox's on the south or Bishop Gardiner's on the north, before you stand between the chantries of Cardinal Beaufort (clearly seen to be a cardinal from his red robes and his red hat) and William of Waynflete. Diagonally opposite Cardinal Beaufort is a rather sickly statue of Joan of Arc, gingerly prodding the air with a sword. Beaufort worked for her downfall and her ultimate burning. Yet they prayed to the same Lord. We can't dismiss this dark side to the history of our faith.

This marvellous space was created by Bishop Godfrey de Lucy in the early thirteenth century. It is thought he may be buried under a modest grey slab just outside the door of the Lady Chapel. What was it for, this space? For processions to form, but also as a special place of pilgrimage and prayer. If you turn to the west you will see nine icons. They are the work of a Russian painter, Sergei Fedorov, who creates icons by the traditional Russian method whereby the act of painting arises out of prayer and is itself a form of prayer.

Each icon sits on two little plinths, each of which once supported a carved figure. Underneath is a small doorway which we call 'the Holy Hole' and above and behind it the place called the Feretory where the relics of saints and kings were once kept. When Lanfranc took over Canterbury he deliberately suppressed the commemoration of many Saxon saints. But here in Winchester Bishop Walkelin and his successors found a place for Saxon saints and kings, perhaps in deference to the mood of a conquered people.

Medieval floor tiles.

Swithun is an oddity to visitors, though locals seem to have got used to him. His statue on the Reredos behind the High Altar shows him holding a bridge and he is certainly remembered for building one. His workmen caused an old lady to drop the eggs she was bringing to market; Swithun rebuked them and the eggs were put back together again miraculously. He was, as he asked, buried outside the Old Minster – the Cathedral while he was Bishop – before appearing to someone in a dream saying he had changed his mind and now wanted to come indoors. When his remains were moved on 15 July 971, forty days of rain followed. So now we have the legend, hardly borne out by experience, that if it is fine on St Swithun's Day it will be fine for forty days, and if it rains it will likewise rain for forty days.

St Swithun's relics were later installed in this place with great ceremony in 1093. However, by contrast with the more popular places of pilgrimage, the shrine does not seem to have attracted great gifts from wealthy pilgrims, at least if the closing-down inventory is anything to go by. The shrine was closed in September 1538 by Henry VIII's men, while the city slept. Some twenty-four cartloads of valuables are said by popular tradition to have been taken from Becket's shrine at Canterbury, yet Swithun was 'our man in heaven', with a following among the less well-heeled and maybe some others.

Here is an ancient prayer to St Swithun:

O father Swithun, our kindly Bishop, through whom the Lord God performed so many wondrous miracles, defend us weak creatures with your paternal presence and protect us with your holy achievements, so that, with your interceding on our behalf as our protector, we may ascend to eternal life. AMEN.

From *The Benedictional of St Aethelwold* (971 -84). This may have been composed by St Aethelwold himself.

Head of a bishop, probably Swithun,
originally in the Great Screen.

The Nine Icons

Now look more closely at the icons. They were dedicated on 25 January 1997 by the Diocesan Bishop and a Russian Orthodox Bishop and made this once again a place of prayer. It's easy to identify the three figures in the centre: Jesus, with his Mother on his right, and John the Baptist on his left. There is an archangel on each side. Then come St Peter (with one scroll) and St Paul (with five). Our local saints flank the others: St Swithun on the north side (that is to say, the right hand side as you look at them) and Birinus on the left. St Birinus is credited with being the first evangelist of Wessex, originally sent by Pope Honorius further west as missionary, but finding the people of Wessex needed sorting out on the way.

You are not standing in front of nine pictures, but nine *icons*. Here is a reminder that you make your prayer in the company of heaven and look towards Christ and reverence him as these icons do. The notice for visitors recalls words of St Stephen the Younger: 'an icon is a door'. You don't need to formulate a prayer in words, but simply 'turn to Christ' in the way demanded by the baptismal service.

The notion of praying 'in the company of heaven' presents us with a wonderful vision. It is like Jacob's dream in which he sees a ladder set up to heaven and angels ascending and descending. The Screen too was a reminder of the Church invisible: here the icons mediate the continuous interchange between heaven and earth through the person of Christ.

Icon of St Birinus.

You may find it helpful to repeat some words which draw on traditional Orthodox prayers and which were composed by Bishop Basil of Sergievo for the consecration of these icons:

Creator and Author of the human race, Giver of all Spiritual grace and Bestower of eternal salvation; send down your Spirit upon us who pray earnestly before these images of your Son and of your Saints; heal us from infirmity and every illness of soul and body, and meet the needs of those for whom we pray, showing thereby your abounding love for humankind. For you are our sanctification, and to you we ascribe glory, to the Father, and the Son and the Holy Spirit, now and forever, and to the ages of ages. AMEN.

The Lady Chapel

Now enter the Lady Chapel. You can see quite clearly where it has been restored. It was originally built by Bishop Godfrey de Lucy at the beginning of the thirteenth century but the restored eastern bay with its badges and decoration comes from the time when the first son of Henry VII and Elizabeth of York was born in Winchester and baptised in the Nave of the Cathedral. They called him Arthur, a name that was a tap-root into the history of Britain, and married him to Katherine of Aragon. He was not much more than a child when he died, the succession and, by Papal permission, his wife passing to his brother, the future Henry VIII.

There must have been many royal visits to Winchester, some of them certainly as ill-omened as Arthur's. Think of William Rufus being brought dead from the New Forest for burial. Here in this same chapel Mary Tudor, Henry VIII's daughter by Katherine of Aragon, married Philip, later King of Spain, an ill-starred marriage which brought no good to either monarch or either country. (Mary's chair is preserved in the Triforium Gallery in the South Transept). But a Lady Chapel is a place where sadness as well as happiness has its place.

We are familiar with the story of the Annunciation, when the angel comes to Mary and declares that she will give birth to the Christchild. Mary responds: 'Be it unto me according to thy will'. Some say it is that initial response, that 'Yes', which makes Mary the type, the forerunner, the first example of the Church which is called into existence as the instrument and agent of God's grace.

In the following prayer King Henry VI offers such obedience, but expresses it within the framework of Christ's saving work.

Lord Jesus Christ, who hast created and redeemed me and hast brought me to that which now I am, thou knowest what thou wouldst do with me, do with me according to thy will, for thy tender mercy's sake. AMEN.

Joys and Sorrows

The three circuits or 'chaplets' of the beads of the rosary reflect first on what are called the 'joyful mysteries', then the 'sorrowful mysteries' and finally the 'glorious mysteries'. They can help us to reflect upon the images of Mary to be found in this place.

First think of Mary the Mother with her Child in her lap, in the joyful mystery of parenthood. Then see the anguished figure of Mary with the dead Christ in her lap (that sorrowful mystery), to the right of the altar here. (It's a piece carved by Peter Eugene Ball and was the gift of some of our Roman Catholic friends who provided it for this Chapel where they sometimes hold services.) Remember the story of Mary meeting her Son risen from the dead and then look up at the ceiling and see in a roof boss the figure of Mary being taken to heaven in glory by angels. The people who could imagine and express the mystery of Mary's glorious ascent were also the people who knew that – for Mary and themselves – the

The Lady Chapel Screen.

griefs and the joys of motherhood were also divine mysteries.

It seemed right when news came of a class of children had been gunned down in Dunblane that people came here and set candles lit in prayer and offering around the Mother grieving over her dead Child.

The Hands that Build – the Statue of William Walker

Leaving the Lady Chapel, turn left and move along to the next Chapel on the south side. To the left of the Chapel is a slim marble pillar topped by the figure of someone in a diving outfit minus the helmet. By it we remember William Walker, a diver who, according to the text and in very truth, 'saved the Cathedral with his own two hands'. In fact the sculptor mistakenly based the figure on the photograph of Francis Fox, the consulting engineer, not the whiskery diver, William Walker.

You can tell the foundations of this end of the Cathedral were uncertain by looking towards the West End along the South Aisle and noticing how the floor curves up and away. In 1905 the East End of the Cathedral was found to be falling away from the rest. The foundations had been laid on logs, which were laid on peat, which lay on the gravel beds beneath. The peat became compressed in some places and quietly leached away in others.

Vast wooden braces were clamped around the building, large numbers of labourers employed and the gaps grouted. But the actual work on the foundations was carried out by this diver. Holes were dug along the foundations but rapidly filled up with water, and it was into this water that he descended, to haul out soggy peat and rotting foundations and to pack in bags of concrete. The approach was primitive but definitely successful. Walker was modest about his work, but was eventually recognised with an MVO.

The name of William Walker is well known to us, but this is the moment to remember and to give thanks for all those who built, cared for and restored this great church in their own time. Maybe it's a help to hear what Ray Course, the Clerk of Works, said in 1997 as he approached his retirement. Holding up his hand with his thumb and forefinger about an inch apart, he said, 'Having responsibility for this building makes you feel so high. I think of all those who have gone before, and the fact that it will go on long after I've gone. There is some marvellous work, and some mistakes – those who worked here before did what seemed right to them and we can only do the same. Sometimes it can seem like a building site, but when the duty Chaplain begins to say the prayers that are said every hour, on the hour, I think "*that's* what it's about" '.

The Cathedral is here thanks to the long continuum of dedicated workmanship by craftsmen who were conscious of being custodians. They too contributed human qualities to the life of the Cathedral community. In giving thanks for this great building, you give thanks for them too.

Those Bones in those Boxes

Start walking back towards the West End, but stop as you come level with the notice referring to the boxes on top of the walls, the ones with bones in them, and take a seat or 'go to the wall' as folk were advised to do when wanting to take the weight off their feet in chairless cathedrals in the old days.

As we have heard, the bones of many Saxon kings and saints – including Birinus and Swithun – were moved from the Old Minster during the hundred or so years following the Norman Conquest. One chronicle states, 'not knowing which were kings and which were bishops, because there were no inscriptions over the monuments, the aforesaid Henry placed in leaden sarcophagi kings and bishops, bishops and kings all mixed together…'

Why did these ancient bones continue to be venerated? Perhaps it was a way in which churches claimed a bit of status. Several said they had the remains of Queen Matilda or Mollde as she was called; royal burials certainly carried a certain cachet. And this was of course a time when the legends and the stories of monarchs, saints and wonderful happenings made up much of popular storytelling.

Boxes and Bones.

The South Transept

Come down now into the South Transept and see in the middle the extraordinary effigy of Samuel Wilberforce being carried into the court of heaven by a posse of angels.

A card displayed on the tomb tells us merely that Bishop Wilberforce is buried at Lavington which is in Sussex. There's a story of some poignancy behind that. A vicar of Lavington, John Sargent, had seven children, five of them daughters. Samuel Wilberforce married Emily Sargent at Lavington in 1828. In 1833 another of the Sargent daughters, Caroline, became engaged and was married eventually to the curate, Mr Henry Manning. Samuel Wilberforce took the wedding. But the Sargent girls suffered a congenital consumptive weakness. Caroline Manning died at Lavington, Samuel and his wife Emily doing what they could to support Henry. But then Emily too died.

The curate had a promising career, becoming Archdeacon of Chichester. To the shock and distress of many he then became a Roman Catholic and, as a widower, was free to be ordained, eventually becoming Cardinal Archbishop of Westminster. His brother-in-law (called 'Soapy' because of an ingratiating manner) had an equally distinguished career in the Church of England. Yet both of them looked back to the Lavington days as to a kind of paradise. In fact Wilberforce was on his way to Lavington when he died. He had taken the train from London to Leatherhead where he and Lord Granville, his companion, took horse to ride the rest of the way. Then Granville, who was riding in front, heard a thump and turning round saw Wilberforce lying motionless. The groom said his horse had stumbled. He lay straight out, his arms at his side in a position described by Granville as 'absolutely monumental'. He was buried alongside the Sargent daughters and their mother in Lavington churchyard.

For all the grandeur of this memorial, it is this story that helps one to say a prayer for Wilberforce. Do you remember your own corner of paradise too? Is this perhaps a place to remember it and its people with thanksgiving?

The Chapel of St John and the Fisherman Apostles

Izaak Walton and the Compleat Anglican

Turn out of the South Transept into the Chapel where Izaak Walton, the fisherman-apostle who, it is said, knew the value of quietness, was buried in 1683. He spent the last five years of his life in the home of his son-in-law, Dr William Hawkins -a prebendary of the Cathedral who lived in No. 7, The Close.

The window in front of you depicts Izaak Walton in two scenes. Bottom left shows Walton at Dovedale in Derbyshire, the scene of many a conversation between Venator and Piscator in Walton's best-known work, *The Compleat Angler*. Bottom right, Walton is in the water meadows at Winchester with St Catherine's Hill in the background.

Higher up in the window are the names of those whose *Lives* Walton wrote. They include John Donne, poet and Dean of St Paul's; Richard Hooker, the ecclesiastical visionary; George Herbert, poet and priest. All exhibited the same strain of Anglicanism as Lancelot Andrewes – neither angularly Protestant nor disdainfully Catholic.

The altar is carved – again by Peter Eugene Ball – from one ton of English oak saved from a tree felled by storm. To prepare this altar for Communion is to lay a picnic on a tree stump in the fluctuating green light of this corner of the Transept. The benches made by Alison Crowther extend the rural theme. Run your hands over the surface of that tree stump in the middle of this clearing which we now call the Chapel of St John the Evangelist and the Fisherman Apostles.

My meaning was, and is, to plant that in your mind, with which I labour to possess my own Soul; that is, a meek and thankful heart. And to that end, I have shew'd you, that riches without them, do not make any man happy. But let me tell you, that riches with them remove many fears, and cares, and therefore my advice is, that you endeavour to be honestly rich; or contentedly poor: *but be sure that your riches be justly got, or you spoil all. For, it is well said by* Caussin, he that loses his conscience, has nothing left that is worth keeping. *Therefore be sure you look to that. And, in the next place, look to your health: and if you have it praise God, and value it next to a good Conscience; for, health is the second blessing that we Mortals are capable of: a blessing, that money cannot buy, and therefore value it, and be thankful for it. As for money (which may be said to be the third blessing) neglect it not: but note, that there is no necessity of being rich. I have heard a grave Divine say, that* God has two dwellings; one in Heaven; and the other in a meek and thankful heart. *Which Almighty God grant to me, and to my honest Scholar.*

Izaak Walton, *The Compleat Angler*, chapter xxi.

The Triforium and the Winchester Bible

Look out for the notices directing you to the Library and the Winchester Bible. Perhaps libraries don't interest you, or your enthusiasm doesn't extend to going up a few stairs. But do yourself a favour and, if you never look at another book in your life, come and look at this one.

Words, the Word and the Word Made Flesh

We are drowning in words. They pour through our letter-boxes, fill up our waste-bins, go soggy in the gutter or blow across wasteland. There seems to be no magic left in them at all. We are doubtful about them – do they reveal or conceal? And yet we also value them. Do you remember the magic of getting a letter and carrying it about with you all day? With words we commit ourselves to one another or struggle to share the things that matter to us. Words bring us together or draw us apart, make peace or war.

Now think of a scribe – a writer in the writers' workshop. Behind the panelling here there is a wall-painting of a scribe from the monastery, whom we call William. For about fifteen years (from say 1160-1175) a scribe like William was working on this Winchester Bible. This was no rapid proliferation of words, tapped up on a screen, printed out, photocopied and mechanically multiplied. Every letter had to be hand-drawn, every word given its place and spacing. He had to design a kind of lettering he could reliably repeat, day after day and which could be read without any perplexity. For these were not just any words, but the words which tell how God and humankind have come together or drifted apart.

William the Scribe.

For Christians, the 'Word of God' consists primarily in the life, death and resurrection of Christ and the ministry of his followers. So we say the Word was 'made flesh'. That Word – expressed here in the Winchester Bible – can heal our lives and make them more creative. Your eye will be caught by the illuminated capital initials, full of foliage and people and activity, but it is the text – wonderfully regular – which most concerns us. Oddly, it also has a connection with the life of modern London.

Calligraphers and those interested in print and lettering are likely to know the name of Edward Johnston. Early this century he gave serious attention to the work of the early scribes, trying to determine what made a 'good' hand. One of Johnston's contemporaries ventured an answer: 'the test of the goodness of a thing is its fitness for that use... if it fails on this first test, no amount of ornamentation or finish will make it any better...' When Johnston was invited by that same man, one of the twentieth-century patrons of art, Frank Pick of London Transport, to design an instantly legible typeface whose forms would flow 'with the full and vigorous rhythms of the great... scribes', he worked with the inspiration of the Winchester Bible. You can still see the lettering that he designed on the destination board of a London bus or the signs in the Underground.

Reformers and Reformation

Before we leave the Library, it is worth reflecting for a moment on the influence which the Bible has had in our history.

The Church was often in need of reformers and was often reformed, but the reformation which so deeply affected English religious life came about when Henry VIII separated from the Papacy. On the surface he did this in order to divorce one wife and marry another, but his reformers plundered the Church and its shrines, discouraged the practice of pilgrimage and closed the monasteries.

In truth the practice of pilgrimage had become discredited. In the late middle ages, two million pilgrims a year – many British – visited Santiago de Compostela in Spain. That's half a million more than the total population of this country at the time of the Domesday Book. Some shrines had become places where tall stories and sharp practices were familiar. Chaucer's tales and other evidence leave us in no doubt that some people went off on so-called pilgrimage for an enjoyable adventure, sometimes of an amorous kind, and neglected their responsibilities. So, surprising as it seems, the end of the pilgrimage business brought minimal fuss from the punters, but considerable loss of revenue to those who kept the shrines.

The suppression of the monasteries was a different matter. Winchester seems to have suffered less than some other cathedral-monasteries; perhaps the monks were more amenable to change. William Kingsmill, the last Prior, became the first Dean of a college of secular canons. But that didn't prevent the legalized theft of the monastery's wealth. And it was Henry's agents who wrought the first damage to the sculpture and ornaments of the Cathedral. Bishop Gardiner's reluctance to change earned him a spell in the Tower of London.

But further damage was done in the Civil War of 1642-8. This was when the medieval glass was shattered. (Some fragments were gathered and have been incorporated into the great West Window.) Priceless manuscripts were taken from the Library and thrown into the river.

The Reformation begun under Henry VIII had put down deep roots into society. There had been an undercurrent of opposition to the defects of the Church, ill-educated clergy preying on superstition, great wealth and power abused. But the movement gained authority when the malcontents laid their hands upon the Bible. By the time of the Civil War, one and a half million copies had been produced and sold or given away in this country. It is commonly said that the Bible was the document of the English Revolution, in contrast with the French Revolution which was fuelled by agnostic or atheist literature. In both cases kings were executed and stability only achieved by the restoration or creation of another monarchy.

By the time Cromwell's soldiers rode their horses through the Cathedral to vandalize the High Altar and all they found, it seemed as if reformation was not to be left to kings, but every man claimed authority as a reformer for himself.

Blessed Lord, who hast caused all holy Scriptures to be written for our learning: Grant that we may in such wise hear them, read, mark, learn, and inwardly digest them, that by patience and comfort of thy holy Word, we may embrace and ever hold fast the blessed hope of everlasting life, which thou hast given us in our Saviour Jesus Christ. AMEN.

The Military Memorials –
the South Aisle

There are more military memorials on the southern side, including regimental memorials. We stand near enough to the conflicts of the twentieth century to read these records with some sense of the occasions and causes in which the soldiers lost their lives. But you may find yourself drawn into more complex and perhaps ambivalent reactions. How do you read the story of the Boer War, or the Crimean? Was the history of the British Empire and the army abroad always and invariably a story of glory? Some ask: 'By having these memorials here in the Cathedral, are you not claiming for them an official righteousness?'

No. Remembrance here is no official seal of approval for any act or any life. It wasn't for the civilians buried here so why should it be for anyone else? But we need to remember. If people are to be sent abroad to risk their lives in what is understood to be the service of their country, they should not be forgotten. With these lists of names our predecessors kept faith with those who did not come back and also with the bereaved. These were local people, and more often, local regiments: the Royal Hampshires, the King's Royal Rifle Corps, the Rifle Brigade.

See how many soldiers died of sickness or failed to recover from wounds. Then reflect that what we tend to get in our history books is the story of campaigns as generals see them. Maybe you are familiar with Charles Wolfe's poem on the burial of Sir John Moore, after the retreat to Corunna in the harsh winter conditions of December 1808 and January

1809. Moore was buried as the force was about to take ship and withdraw.

> We thought, as we hollowed his narrow bed
> And smoothed down his lonely pillow,
> That the foe and the stranger would tread
> O'er his head, and we far away on the billow.

But the account of that retreat by an ordinary rifleman tells of the harshness and savagery and the great loss of life. Are they just names? Take one list and read to yourself the names of the first half dozen. Try to imagine them as human beings like ourselves, with a place of origin – perhaps local – to which they didn't return. Just names, perhaps, but here they are remembered.

The Extravagance of God

> More sky than man can see,
> More seas than he can sail
> More sun than he can bear to watch,
> More stars than he can scale.
>
> More breath than he can breathe,
> More yield than he can sow,
> More grace than he can comprehend,
> More love than he can know.

Ralph W. Seager

Last Thoughts and First

As we come towards the West Doors of the Cathedral on the return journey, we are back with the question 'What is this place for?' We have found it to be a place where prayers are offered daily, morning and evening, but not just at the publicized times of services. People are praying here throughout the day and the building itself suggests an attitude of continuous prayer.

The prayer offered is for the world – whether or not the world knows about it or cares; it is for the people who come here – whether or not at their express request – and for those who never enter any church; it is prayer within the company of heaven, as we discovered in front of the High Altar and the icons. It is a place where we remember those we have known and keep them before God. It's a place where people come with the joyful, sorrowful and glorious mysteries of their lives, to place them in the keeping of the Lord of all mysteries. It is a threshold place, a place where we seek God.

The people who built this place and have worshipped here believed that God came seeking us and still does. He still uses this space – it is his dedicated 'highway'. He will meet us here, we may depend upon it:

Herein is love, not that we love God but that he first loved us.
1 John 4. 11

With that we have come to the heart of it at last. Do you remember how I said that the Church began when Mary heard the gracious word of God and replied: 'Be it unto me according to thy will'? This building was begun, built, rebuilt, refashioned, adorned, made glorious as a human response to the overwhelming, continuing and teeming generosity of God. In the same way in the New Testament a woman comes to the feast where Christ is a guest, breaks a box of precious ointment over his feet and wipes it away with her tears. As Charles Simeon (d. 1836), a great preacher, wrote, 'Who can see a true Christian without being impressed by the love, mercy and forgiveness which have been shown towards him?'

Look at the woman in the story above and wonder at the love which inspired her generosity. Look at this building and know the greatness of the love, mercy and forgiveness which have been shown towards us.

Sometimes people grumble a bit about being asked to contribute to the upkeep of places like Winchester. Grudged gifts are no gifts. But as we share a sense of God's ungrudging generosity to us, maybe we begin to live a more generous life ourselves.

To God the Father, who first loved us, and made us accepted in the beloved; to God the Son, who loved us, and washed us from our sins in his own blood; to God the Holy Ghost, who sheds the love of God abroad in our hearts; to the one true God be all love and all glory, for time and for eternity.

Thomas Ken (1637–1711)
Canon of Winchester,
Bishop of Bath and Wells